EDGE BOOKS

WAR MACHINES — DESTROYERS

The Arleigh Burke Class

by Michael and Gladys Green

Consultant:
Lieutenant Matthew Galan
Public Affairs Officer
Navy Office of Information, New York City

Edge Books are published by Capstone Press
151 Good Counsel Drive, P.O. Box 669, Mankato, Minnesota 56002
www.capstonepress.com

Library of Congress Cataloging-in-Publication Data
Green, Michael, 1952–
    Destroyers: the Arleigh Burke class / by Michael and Gladys Green.
    p. cm.—(Edge books. War machines)
    Includes bibliographical references and index.
    ISBN 0-7368-2722-6 (hardcover)
    1. Destroyers (Warships)—United States—Juvenile literature. 2. Arleigh Burke
(Destroyer)—Juvenile literature. I. Green, Gladys, 1954– II. Title. III. Series.
V825.3.G7423 2005
623.825'4—dc22   2004001342

Summary: Describes the Arleigh Burke destroyer, including its history, equipment,
weapons, tactics, and future use with the U.S. Navy.

Editorial Credits
Katy Kudela, editor; Jason Knudson, series designer; Molly Nei, book designer;
    Jo Miller, photo researcher; Eric Kudalis, product planning editor

Photo Credits
DVIC, 22; BIW/Debbie Huston, 12; PH2 Felix Garza, 14; PH3 Chris Vickers, 25;
    PH3 Jeffery Bush, 8–9
Fotodynamics/Ted Carlson, 16–17
Getty Images Inc./Newsmakers/Lockheed Martin, 11; Newsmakers/U.S. Navy, 5
Photo courtesy of Northrop Grumman Litton Ingalls Shipbuilding, cover
U.S. Naval Historical Center Photograph/Collection of C. A. Shively, 6
U.S. Navy photo, 21; PH2 Dennis C. Cantrell, 29; PH3 Ramon Preciado, 19;
    U.S. Navy Graphic, 27

1 2 3 4 5 6 09 08 07 06 05 04

Table of Contents

CHAPTER 1

The Arleigh Burke in Action

A U.S. Arleigh Burke destroyer sails off the coast of an enemy country. The destroyer is protecting a group of Navy supply ships. The destroyer's computer locates three enemy planes.

The pilots of the enemy planes discover they have been spotted on radar. The enemy planes launch six antiship missiles. The Arleigh Burke destroyer's crew then launches guided missiles. The missiles quickly shoot down the antiship missiles and the enemy planes.

The sonar system on the destroyer then finds an enemy submarine. The ship's crew launches a guided missile. The missile shoots into the air and then drops into the ocean. The missile destroys the enemy sub. The destroyer and supply ships continue to sail.

The U.S. Navy's newest class of destroyers is the Arleigh Burke.

LEARN ABOUT:

Protecting Navy ships

Arleigh Burke history

Design of Arleigh Burke

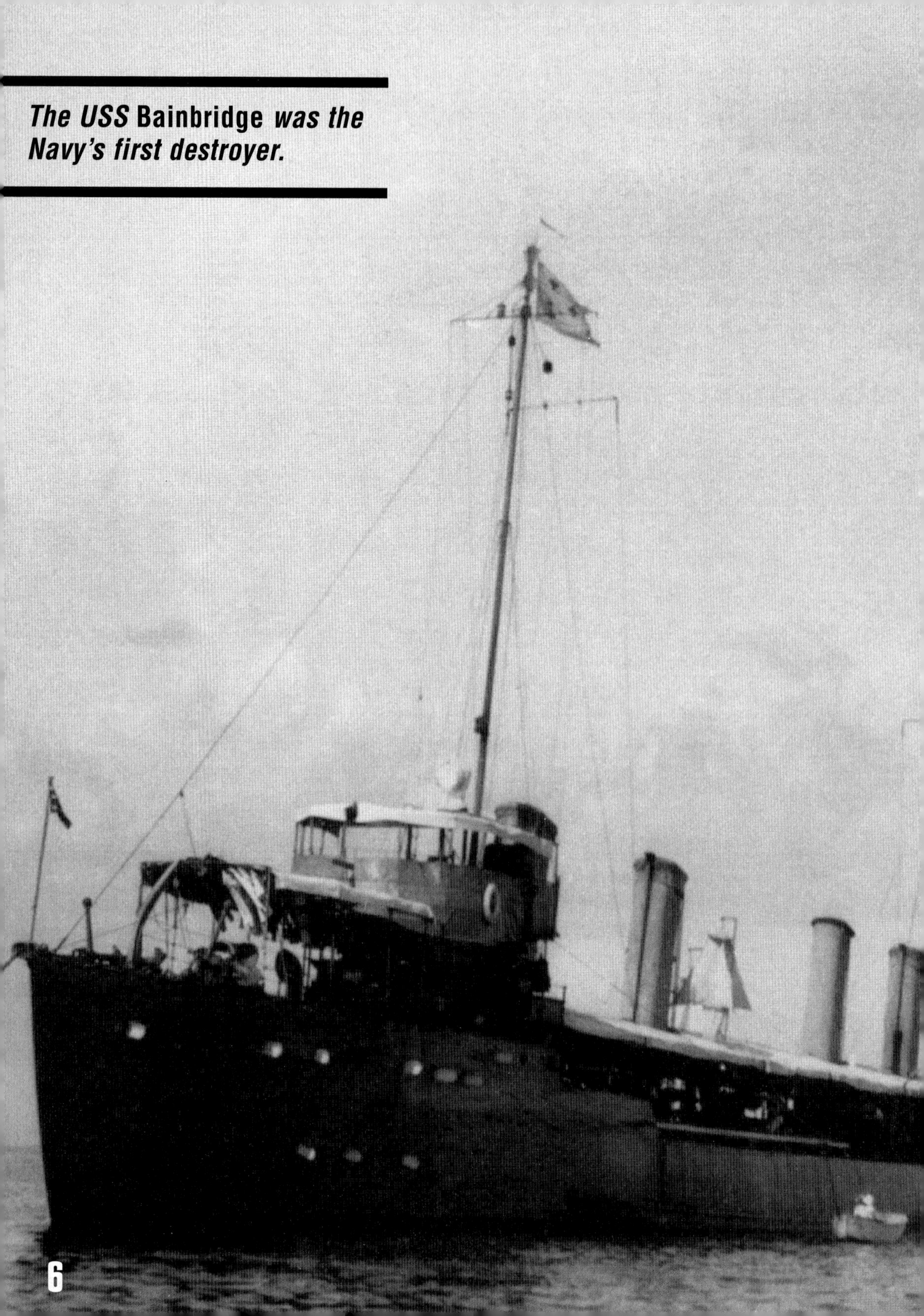

The USS Bainbridge *was the Navy's first destroyer.*

Building Navy Destroyers

The U.S. Navy's first destroyer was the USS *Bainbridge*. This ship entered Navy service in 1901. The *Bainbridge* was the lead ship in a class of 16 destroyers.

The *Bainbridge* and other early destroyers were built to sink enemy subs. During World War I (1914–1918), these ships sank enemy subs and guarded cargo ships.

After World War I, the demand for destroyers in the U.S. Navy grew. Since World War II (1939–1945), U.S. shipyards have built hundreds of destroyers for the U.S. Navy.

In 1979, the U.S. Navy started plans for a new class of destroyers. Shipbuilders added thick steel to the ships. Bulletproof material was also added to the ships. These materials protected the ships from enemy weapons.

The first ship in the Arleigh Burke class was named the USS *Arleigh Burke*. It entered Navy service in 1991. The Arleigh Burke class is the newest class of Navy destroyers in service.

The U.S. Navy continues to update the design of its Arleigh Burke destroyers. The Navy's newest

Arleigh Burke destroyers have added features. Earlier destroyers had a rear flight deck but no hangar to store a helicopter. The Navy's newest Arleigh Burke destroyers have two hangars. This updated design makes it possible for the destroyers to store two helicopters.

The USS Arleigh Burke *entered Navy service in 1991.*

CHAPTER 2

Inside the Arleigh Burke

One of the major sections of an Arleigh Burke destroyer is the hull. The hull, or main body, of the ship is made of steel. Many decks, or floors, divide the ship's hull.

The superstructure is the other main part of a destroyer. It is a large metal building with many decks and windows. It sits on top of the hull.

Near the front of the superstructure is the ship's bridge. The captain commands the ship from the bridge. On top of the superstructure is a mast. A mast is a tall pole that supports the ship's antennas.

The hull of an Arleigh Burke is made of thick steel.

LEARN ABOUT:

Superstructure

Locating enemy subs

Power behind destroyers

Combat Information Center

The Combat Information Center (CIC) is an important area on an Arleigh Burke. An Aegis Combat System is at the center of the CIC. This computer system controls the ship's radar and guided missiles. The system keeps track of missiles launched from the destroyer. It can change the missiles' flight paths to make sure they hit the targets.

ARLEIGH BURKE

Sonar Systems

Arleigh Burke destroyers carry two sonar systems. Sonar helps the ship's crew find and track enemy subs.

A destroyer's main sonar system is the AN/SQS-53C. It is located at the front of the ship. The sonar sends out powerful sound waves through the water. Sound waves that find a submarine bounce back to the ship. The sonar operators receive an alert signal.

Arleigh Burke destroyers also have the SQR-19 Tactical Towed Array Sonar (TACTAS). This sonar is kept at the back of a destroyer. The TACTAS is a long cable with microphones attached to the end. The cable is towed behind the ship. The microphones pick up sounds.

Power Source

An Arleigh Burke has two propellers. These propellers move the ship through the water. Four gas turbine engines power the propellers. These engines give the ship a top speed of about 35 miles (56 kilometers) per hour.

An Arleigh Burke destroyer is equipped with two propellers.

The gas turbine engines in an Arleigh Burke take only minutes to come to full power. They are quieter than engines on other Navy warships. A quieter engine makes it easier for the destroyer's sonar to pick up sounds.

Crew members examine a destroyer's gas turbine engine.

Air Protection

The U.S. Navy built the Arleigh Burke class destroyers to operate in poor air conditions. Poor air conditions might result from nuclear weapons or chemicals used during battle.

Arleigh Burke destroyers have few doors that open to the outside of the ship. This design helps protect the crew from bad air. Double air-locked doors also help to keep outside air from entering the ship.

Arleigh Burke destroyers have filters to clean the air inside the ship. An air system also keeps the air moving.

The Arleigh Burke Class

Function:	Warship
Manufacturer:	Bath Iron Works, Ingalls Shipbuilding
Date First Deployed:	1991
Length, overall:	505 to 510 feet (154 to 155 meters)
Width:	67 feet (20 meters)
Power Source:	Four gas turbine engines
Top Speed:	About 35 miles (56 kilometers) per hour
Crew:	23 officers, 300 enlisted members

1 Hull

2 MK-45 gun

3 Superstructure

4 Mast

5 Antennas

6 Helicopter pad

CHAPTER 3

Weapons and Tactics

Arleigh Burke destroyers carry weapons for each job they perform. A destroyer has guided missiles, torpedoes, and guns. This equipment is used to protect aircraft carriers and ground troops.

Guns and Weapon Systems

Arleigh Burke destroyers have an MK-45 gun. The MK-45 is at the front of the ship. The gun has a range of about 13 miles (21 kilometers). Navy crews use it to attack enemy ships, planes, and land targets.

The MK-45 gun fires from the front of a destroyer.

LEARN ABOUT:

Weapon systems

Missiles

Carrier strike group

19

Each destroyer has two MK 15 Phalanx Close-In Weapon Systems (CIWS). The CIWS has radar. It also has a gun, a bullet storage space, and a computer. Destroyers use the weapon system against enemy planes and antiship missiles.

Guided Missiles

Guided missiles are the most important weapons on Arleigh Burke destroyers. An Arleigh Burke carries three different kinds of guided missiles. A destroyer's crew uses these missiles against land and sea targets.

Missiles are stored and launched from two launcher boxes in the ship's hull. The missiles and launchers are part of the MK 41 Vertical Launching System. The launcher boxes are located at the front and back of the ship.

Tomahawk missiles are launched from destroyers.

Harpoon missiles can destroy enemy ships.

The Tomahawk Land Attack Missile destroys land targets. It has a range of more than 600 miles (966 kilometers). The missile travels 550 miles (885 kilometers) per hour.

A destroyer's crew uses the Standard SM-2 guided missile to shoot down aircraft and missiles. This missile is about 15 feet (5 meters) long. It has a top range of 100 miles (161 kilometers).

The Vertical Launch RUR-5 ASROC missile destroys enemy subs. This missile has a homing torpedo attached to a rocket motor. The homing torpedo guides the missile to the enemy sub.

Other Weapons

An Arleigh Burke carries eight Harpoon antiship guided missiles. These missiles are located at the back of the hull. The top range of Harpoon missiles is 67 miles (108 kilometers). A destroyer's crew uses these missiles against nearby enemy ships.

Destroyers also carry torpedoes that are used against enemy subs. An Arleigh Burke has MK-46 lightweight torpedoes. Crew members fire these torpedoes from launchers at the back of the ship. They have a range of about 7 miles (11 kilometers).

Missions

Arleigh Burke class destroyers are used in many missions. A destroyer can be part of a carrier strike group. In this role, a destroyer helps protect an aircraft carrier. Destroyers use radar to search for enemy planes. They use sonar to search for enemy subs.

Arleigh Burke destroyers perform missions to protect supply ships. The supply ships bring fuel, food, and ammunition to Navy carrier strike groups.

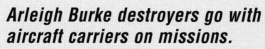
Arleigh Burke destroyers go with aircraft carriers on missions.

CHAPTER 4

The Future

Today, the U.S. Navy continues to add Arleigh Burke destroyers to its fleet. The newest destroyer will be the USS *Farragut*. More ships will follow in the coming years.

DDX Destroyers

In 2001, the Department of Defense announced plans for a new class of destroyers. The name of this class is DDX multimission destroyers. The U.S. Navy plans to use DDX destroyers in shallow coastal waters. The destroyers will provide support for ground forces.

LEARN ABOUT:

New Arleigh Burke

DDX design

Design updates

Updated Design

The Navy plans to give DDX destroyers a new design. These destroyers will have a lower hull and superstructure. This design will make it more difficult for enemies to spot the ship.

The Navy plans to use more computer equipment on its DDX destroyers. More computer equipment will lower the number of crew members needed to operate the ships. Fewer crew members will make these destroyers less expensive to operate. A smaller crew will also provide more room for weapons.

The U.S. Navy plans to use the DDX destroyers to replace the ships built before the Arleigh Burke class. The Arleigh Burke class destroyers will continue to protect aircraft carriers and other warships throughout the ocean. They will remain in U.S. Navy service for many years.

Arleigh Burke class destroyers have a strong future with the U.S. Navy.

Glossary

ammunition (am-yuh-NISH-uhn)—rounds, missiles, and other objects that can be fired from weapons

fleet (FLEET)—a group of warships under one command

hangar (HANG-ur)—a large sheltered area where aircraft are parked and maintained

hull (HULL)—the main body of a ship

missile (MISS-uhl)—an explosive weapon that can fly long distances

propeller (pruh-PEL-ur)—a set of rotating blades that provides thrust to move a ship through water

radar (RAY-dar)—equipment that uses radio waves to locate and guide objects

superstructure (SOO-per-struhk-chur)—the part of a ship that rises above the main deck

torpedo (tor-PEE-doh)—an explosive weapon that travels underwater

turbine engine (TUR-bine EN-juhn)—an engine powered by steam or gas; the steam or gas moves through the blades of a fanlike device and makes it turn.

Read More

Baldwin, Carol, and Ron Baldwin. *Navy Fighting Vessels.* U.S. Armed Forces. Chicago: Heinemann, 2004.

Cooper, Jason. *U.S. Navy.* Fighting Forces. Vero Beach, Fla.: Rourke, 2004.

Dartford, Mark. *Warships.* Military Hardware in Action. Minneapolis: Lerner, 2003.

Internet Sites

FactHound offers a safe, fun way to find Internet sites related to this book. All of the sites on FactHound have been researched by our staff.

Here's how:

1. Visit *www.facthound.com*
2. Type in this special code **0736827226** for age-appropriate sites. Or enter a search word related to this book for a more general search.
3. Click on the **Fetch It** button.

FactHound will fetch the best sites for you!

Index